NEW ZEALAND

eye on the landscape

NEW ZEALAND

eye on the landscape

craig potton publishing

PREFACE

A few years ago a catalogue from a landscape photography competition in Christchurch crossed my desk. I was stopped in my tracks by a particularly beautiful photo on the cover, but because I don't move in the world of photographic clubs, the photographer responsible for this image was unknown to me. The artistry of the image was easy to see however, and sparked an idea.

It struck me that there was probably a sizeable pool of largely unseen, but very, very good landscape photography being generated by the clearly passionate members of the many photographic clubs in New Zealand. And my hunch was that the best of these images could well make a book of New Zealand landscape photography of the highest quality. Happily this idea met with enthusiastic support from the Photographic Society of New Zealand (the national body for all photographic clubs in New Zealand) and we subsequently sought submissions from members of the PSNZ, who range from full-time professionals to part-time amateurs.

New Zealand: Eye on the Landscape is the result. With my colleague, photographer Craig Potton, we selected the photographs within some simple parameters. We wanted a book that would reach beyond those only interested in the art of photography, to both locals and visitors who were seeking a book about the remarkable landscape we have in this country. This meant that we needed a comprehensive geographic spread through both islands. It also meant that we concentrated on photos that gave us a wider view of the land, rather than than those focused on abstract detail or pattern.

But ultimately we were interested in strong work, and to our delight, we found plenty of that. For two decades in my role as a publisher of New Zealand landscape books and calendars, I have looked every year at many, many thousands of images, and so I was also amazed at the fresh and original photographs that appeared – many of the images we selected are of places I have never seen photographed well before.

I was also intrigued by the places that grab the imagination of this particular group of photographers. The clear winners were the big skies and bony hills of Central Otago and the Mackenzie Country, which seem to have a strong appeal to our photographic community, while Lake Alexandrina, the small lake next to Lake Tekapo, took out the prize for the most photographed part of New Zealand by those submitting for this book.

It has turned out to be an enormously rewarding task putting together *Eye on the Landscape*. Not only is there the real aesthetic pleasure of working with an inspired and well-made photograph, but in the end it is the landscape itself that comes shining through this collection of images. Here there is a simple, uncomplicated truth for me – I want a landscape photograph to transport me. I want to feel the chill of a southerly change, with the cloud lifting and light lying over a high-country lake. I want to be back on the cliffs above a West Coast beach as a late-summer sun slips into the ocean. And every time a photograph has the heart to do this, then I know that what the photographers in this book are chasing is truly worthwhile.

ROBBIE BURTON
CO-OWNER AND PUBLISHER
CRAIG POTTON PUBLISHING

ABOVE Morning light on the western faces of Mt Tasman, New Zealand's second-highest mountain, Westland/Tai Poutini National Park. A. JOHN V. HART

OPPOSITE Mt Tasman and Aoraki/Mt Cook reflected in Lake Matheson, near Fox Glacier, Westland/Tai Poutini National Park. JUSTINA YONG

ABOVE A recent ice collapse at the terminal of the Fox Glacier, the source of the Fox River, Westland/Tai Poutini National Park. GRAHAM DAINTY

OPPOSITE The Waiho River flows out from under the terminal of the Franz Josef Glacier, Westland/Tai Poutini National Park. SAMUEL CHAN

OVERLEAF Cattle graze in the evening light on flats near Fox Glacier, South Westland. THIERRY HUET

Morning sun rises over river flats near Lake Matheson, South Westland. DAVID BECKINGHAM

On a still winter's morning mist lies around the forested fringe of Lake Mapourika, just north of Franz Josef, Westland/Tai Poutini National Park. RICHARD SIMMONDS

ABOVE The Pancake Rocks and blowholes at Dolomite Point, Punakaiki, Paparoa National Park. CHRIS LOUSICH

OPPOSITE A sou'westerly swell drives into rocks near Punakaiki, Paparoa National Park. TONI WILSON

Coastal rimu forest running down to the beach at Bruce Bay, South Westland. THIERRY HUET

Tree ferns in forest near the Moria Gate Arch, Oparara Valley near Karamea, Kahurangi National Park. STEPHEN WRIGHT

Creek flowing into the sea near Kohaihai at the southern end of the Heaphy Track, West Coast. STEPHEN WRIGHT

Dusk at Gillespies Beach, with Mt Tasman and Aoraki/Mt Cook on the skyline, South Westland. RICHARD SIMMONDS

ABOVE A nor'wester blows down the Dart River near Paradise, Glenorchy, Mount Aspiring National Park. JUSTINA YONG

OPPOSITE Poplar trees catching the autumn sun near Albert Town, Central Otago. DAVID BECKINGHAM

OVERLEAF The historic village of Saint Bathans sits alongside Blue Lake, formed in the aftermath of gold mining excavation, Central Otago. GRAHAM DAINTY

ABOVE Old gold diggings near Bannockburn, Central Otago. DAVID BECKINGHAM

OPPOSITE A vineyard on a terrace above the Kawarau River, Gibbston Valley near Queenstown, Central Otago. RICHARD SIMMONDS

ABOVE Autumn colour in forest above the Arrow River, Arrowtown, Central Otago. ANDIE PRYCE

OPPOSITE The tussock and schist landscape of Danseys Pass, Central Otago. A. JOHN V. HART

ABOVE The Clutha River at Albert Town, near Wanaka, Central Otago. RON WILLEMS

OPPOSITE A calm morning at the southern end of Lake Hawea, Central Otago. A. JOHN V. HART

WEDDERBURN

ABOVE Autumn at the southern end of Lake Wanaka, Central Otago. JOHN HODGSON

OPPOSITE The old Wedderburn Railway goods shed in Central Otago, immortalised in Grahame Sydney's 1975 painting. JIM GRAYDON

Sunlight hits the shore of Lake Hayes, near Queenstown, Central Otago. DAVID BECKINGHAM

Autumn colour above the Shotover River, near Queenstown, Central Otago. RON McKIE

ABOVE Cloud over Blue Lake, Saint Bathans, Central Otago. JEAN MOULIN

OPPOSITE Old cottage amid low snow, Maniototo, Central Otago. RON PARRY

ABOVE Snowfall at Butchers Dam, south of Alexandra, Central Otago. KIM ANNAN

OPPOSITE Hoar frost at Fruitlands, between Alexandra and Roxburgh, Central Otago. A. JOHN V. HART

ABOVE Lake Wanaka from Treble Cone Skifield, Central Otago. THIERRY HUET

OPPOSITE Lake Wakatipu from The Remarkables, near Queenstown, Central Otago. STEVE BOLT

Autumn at Glendhu Bay, Lake Wanaka, Central Otago. MATHESON BEAUMONT

Cloud over hills near Tarras, Central Otago. MATHESON BEAUMONT

ABOVE Waterfalls after rain, Milford Sound, Fiordland National Park. RYAN NIELSON

OPPOSITE Low tide at Milford Sound, Fiordland National Park. GRAHAM DAINTY

OVERLEAF Beech forest on the Cascade Creek Nature Walk near Lake Gunn, Eglinton Valley, Fiordland National Park. GRAHAM DAINTY

ABOVE Low light in Doubtful Sound, Fiordland National Park. NEWELL GRENFELL

OPPOSITE An aerial view above the head of Milford Sound, with Mitre Peak on the left, and spray from the Bowen Falls obvious on the right, Fiordland National Park. GRAHAM DAINTY

Morning sun in beech forest on the Milford Road, Eglinton Valley, Fiordland National Park. GRAHAM DAINTY

ABOVE Head of the Cleddau Valley on the Milford Road above Milford Sound, Fiordland National Park. GRAHAM DAINTY

OVERLEAF The McKinnon Memorial on top of Mackinnon Pass, which lies between the Clinton and Arthur valleys on the Milford Track, Fiordland National Park. GRAHAM DAINTY

ABOVE Late evening over Lake Manapouri, Fiordland National Park. RYAN NIELSON

OPPOSITE A rainbow in Dusky Sound, Fiordland National Park. CHRIS PIPER

ABOVE A stormy day at the Moeraki Boulders, north of Dunedin. SIMON WOOLF

OPPOSITE Windshorn shelterbelt, Slope Point, Southland. KIM ANNAN

The multi-tiered Purakaunui Falls on the Purakaunui River, The Catlins. JOANNE McLEARY

The Nugget Point Lighthouse, with The Nuggets below, near Kaka Point, The Catlins. MEGAN INWOOD

The sandstone cliffs at Tunnel Beach, southwest of Dunedin. RYAN NIELSON

A double rainbow on the beach at Ocean View, southwest of Dunedin. A. JOHN V. HART

ABOVE Sunrise over podocarp forest above Papatowai, The Catlins. DAVID BECKINGHAM

OPPOSITE Storm clouds over the Otago Harbour, seen from Macandrew Bay, near Dunedin. CHRIS HEWITT

ABOVE Morning sun on yachts moored near Port Chalmers, Otago Harbour, Dunedin. RON WILLEMS

OPPOSITE Tussock hills near the Lindis Pass, Otago. ANNE TATE

ABOVE Snow on the Gamack Range above the rolling Mackenzie Country, between Lake Tekapo and Lake Pukaki. RON WILLEMS

OPPOSITE Sunset on the western side of the Lindis Pass, Otago. A. JOHN V. HART

ABOVE Tussock on the approach to the Lindis Pass from the Mackenzie Country. BRUCE BURGESS

OPPOSITE The entrance to Irishman Creek Station, Mackenzie Country. RON PARRY

ABOVE Last light on the south face of Aoraki/Mt Cook, Aoraki/Mount Cook National Park. NEWELL GRENFELL

OPPOSITE Winter sunset and nor'west cloud above Lake Pukaki and Aoraki/Mt Cook, Mackenzie Country. ELIZABETH CARRUTHERS

ABOVE Looking down the Hooker Valley toward the head of Lake Pukaki, Aoraki/Mount Cook National Park. GRANT NEWTON

OPPOSITE High cloud above Lake Alexandrina, Mackenzie Country. NICKI MAUD

Ben Ohau, from the shores of Lake Ohau, Mackenzie Country. A. JOHN V. HART

Clearing storm, Lake Clearwater, Canterbury high country. RYAN NIELSON

Spring snowfall near Lindis Pass, Otago. JOHN BOYD

Hoar frost on trees beside Lake Pearson, Canterbury high country. MATHESON BEAUMONT

ABOVE The foothills of the Southern Alps on the road between Lake Coleridge and Lake Lyndon, Canterbury high country. RICHARD SIMMONDS

OPPOSITE The Canterbury Plains seen from the Mt Hutt access road, with the Rakaia River leading out to the coast. RON McKIE

ABOVE The historic Waiau Ferry Bridge near Hanmer, North Canterbury. COLLEEN CARROLL

OPPOSITE The lower entrance of the cave through which Cave Stream flows, Castle Hill Basin, Canterbury high country. JOHN C. SMITH

Autumn at the Acheron Accommodation House, built out of cob in 1863, Molesworth Station, North Canterbury. KAY JACKSON

Vineyard at Dillons Point near Blenheim, Marlborough. DAVID BRINN

ABOVE Sawcut Gorge, Isolated Hill Scenic Reseve, Marlborough. DON PITTHAM

OPPOSITE Evening in Kenepuru Sound, Marlborough Sounds. THIERRY HUET

ABOVE Spring growth in the Buller Gorge, West Coast. RON WILLEMS

OPPOSITE Mist clears after fresh snow, Lake Rotoiti, Nelson Lakes National Park. RON WILLEMS

ABOVE Winter evening, Nelson Haven, Nelson. TONI WILSON

OPPOSITE The sweep of Totaranui Beach from Skinner Point, Abel Tasman National Park. KAY JACKSON

ABOVE Inside Ngarua Cave on top of Takaka Hill, between Nelson and Golden Bay. GRANT NEWTON

OPPOSITE Dawn on the beach at Collingwood, Golden Bay. GRANT NEWTON

ABOVE Sand dunes on Farewell Spit, Golden Bay. CHRIS PIPER

OPPOSITE The Archway Islands off Wharariki Beach, Golden Bay. BARRY WHITNALL

Island Bay, with the sun setting over the distant South Island, Wellington. SHONA JARAY

Kapiti Island, seen from Waikanae Beach, Kapiti Coast. SHONA JARAY

ABOVE A southerly front rolling in at Deliverance Cove, Castlepoint, Wairarapa Coast. JIM GRAYDON

OPPOSITE Sunrise over the Castlepoint Lighthouse, Wairarapa Coast. JEREMY BRIGHT

OVERLEAF The Tararua Ranges, seen from near Masterton, Wairarapa. SHONA JARAY

ABOVE A rural lane near Havelock North, Hawke's Bay. MEG LIPSCOMBE

OPPOSITE Turnoff to Ngamatea Station, Gentle Annie Road, between Napier and Taihape. MEG LIPSCOMBE

OVERLEAF A country church at Opaea, near Taihape, Central North Island. JEREMY BRIGHT

ABOVE & OPPOSITE Papa cliffs on the Whanganui River up-river from Pipiriki, Whanganui National Park. MARK BRIMBLECOMBE

ABOVE House in river mist, Jerusalem, Whanganui River. LEONIE CADMAN

OPPOSITE Sheep on the road, Makakahi Valley, Raetihi, Central North Island. LEONIE CADMAN

OVERLEAF Mt Taranaki and the Pouakai Range at sunset, seen from Tongaporutu, North Taranaki. ANNE TATE

ABOVE The lighthouse at Cape Egmont in Taranaki was first lit in 1881. JEAN MOULIN

OPPOSITE The volcanic cone of Mt Taranaki, at the centre of Egmont National Park. ELIZABETH CARRUTHERS

ABOVE Mt Taranaki at sunset, seen from Tongariro National Park, Central North Island. ROGER BROWNSEY

OPPOSITE A winter view of the distant summits of Mt Ruapehu and Mt Ngauruhoe, from near the settlement of Peep-o-Day, Northern Manawatu. STEVE JOHNSON

ABOVE Ratana Church near Raetihi, Central North Island. KIMBER BROWN

OPPOSITE Farmland on the Parapara highway between Raetihi and Whanganui. LEONIE CADMAN

ABOVE Mt Ruapehu in winter, seen from the west, Central North Island. LEONIE CADMAN

OPPOSITE The Chateau and Whakapapa Village in winter, Mt Ruapehu, Tongariro National Park. SHONA KEBBLE

ABOVE A lenticular cloud caps the summit of Mt Ngauruhoe, Tongariro National Park. JEREMY BRIGHT

OPPOSITE Winter on Pinnacle Ridge, Mt Ruapehu, looking toward the summits of Mts Tongariro and Ngauruhoe, Tongariro National Park. BRIDGET WINSTONE

OVERLEAF A yacht slowly crosses Lake Taupo, with the volcanoes of Tongariro National Park rising up in the distance. JEREMY BRIGHT

ABOVE Looking south over the Crater Lake on the summit of Mt Ruapehu, Tongariro National Park. JEREMY BRIGHT

OPPOSITE The Mahuia Rapids on the Whakapapanui River, Tongariro National Park. RODNEY DUGMORE

ABOVE Farmland above Makorori Beach, just north of Gisborne. RAEWYNE CATHIE

OPPOSITE Sunrise behind the Anglican Church at Raukokore, near Cape Runaway on the east coast of the North Island. JASON BYRNE

LEFT The 55-metre drop of Waireinga/Bridal Veil Falls, on the Pakoka River near Raglan, Waikato. RODNEY DUGMORE

OPPOSITE Ferns and forest alongside the Mangakara Sream, Pirongia Forest Park, Waikato. RODNEY DUGMORE

ABOVE The erupting mud pool at Waiotapu, reputedly New Zealand's largest, near Rotorua. BRUCE BURGESS

OPPOSITE The internationally renowned Champagne Pool at Waiotapu, geothermally heated and coloured by mineral salts, near Rotorua. BRUCE BURGESS

ABOVE The huge fissure formed in the summit of Mt Tarawera after it erupted in1886, near Rotorua. MEG LIPSCOMBE

OPPOSITE Steaming fumaroles on Whakaari or White Island, New Zealand's only active marine volcano, Bay of Plenty. BRUCE BURGESS

ABOVE Te Hoho, the prominent sea stack at Cathedral Cove, near Hahei, Coromandel Peninsula. KIM ANNAN

OPPOSITE Pohutukawa tree and stony beach north of Kaiaua, on the Firth of Thames. KIMBER BROWN

Looking through the cave that links Mare's Leg and Cathedral coves, near Hahei, Coromandel Peninsula. ROGER BROWNSEY

Looking toward the coast out from Aotea Harbour, with Mt Karioi in the distance, Waikato. MALCOLM LYONS

ABOVE Dawn on the Waihou River, near Turua on the Hauraki Plains, inland from Thames. JUDITH BISHOP

OPPOSITE Jetty at Hamurana on the shores of Lake Rotorua, near Rotorua. JASON BYRNE

ABOVE An aerial view of Little Barrier Island (Hauturu) from above Aotea/Great Barrier Island, Hauraki Gulf. MALCOLM LYONS

OPPOSITE Dawn spreads over Auckland City and Rangitoto Island, seen from the top of One Tree Hill. SHONA JARAY

The sun sets into the Tasman Sea beyond the gannet colony at Muriwai on Auckland's west coast. RODNEY DUGMORE

Pohutukawa trees at sunset on Little Barrier Island (Hauturu), Hauraki Gulf. BRIDGET WINSTONE

ABOVE Evening over the Sky Tower and downtown Auckland, from the Viaduct Basin. PAM RUSSELL

OPPOSITE Low tide at Piha, with Lion Rock behind, Auckland's west coast. BRUCE BURGESS

ABOVE A fisherman surfcasting off rocks at Muriwai, on Auckland's west coast. DON McLEOD

OPPOSITE A grove of kauri on the Manginangina Walkway, Puketi Forest, Northland. DON PITTHAM

ABOVE Looking south on Te Henga Walkway, which runs north from Bethells Beach to near Muriwai, on Auckland's west coast. RODNEY DUGMORE

OPPOSITE Rocks at Farley Point, Karekare, on Auckland's west coast. RODNEY DUGMORE

OVERLEAF Sunset at Russell, Bay of Islands, Northland. STEPHEN WESTERN

Early morning mist on the waterfront at Russell, Bay of Islands. STEPHEN WESTERN

ABOVE The lighthouse at Cape Reinga, illuminated by moonlight. ANNE TATE

OPPOSITE A fishing boat rounds Cape Reinga, at the northern end of the North Island, widely considered to be the dividing line between the Tasman Sea and the Pacific Ocean. JENNY DEY

First published in 2010 by Craig Potton Publishing

Craig Potton Publishing
98 Vickerman Street, PO Box 555, Nelson, New Zealand
www.craigpotton.co.nz

ISBN: 978 1 877517 36 5

Printed in China by Midas Printing International Ltd